THE POTTER'S DESIRE

Mercy Asare

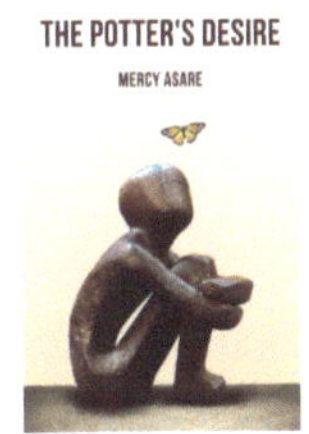

ISBN: 9798862386554

Cover design by Canva
Library of Congress Control Number: 2018675309
Printed in the United States of America

CONTENTS

Introduction:

(The Searcher)

There's an ancient parable Potter who molds clay into magnificent vessels. Each piece is uniquely shaped and designed for a specific purpose, mirroring our relationship with the Divine Potter - God. This book, "The Potter's Desire," delves into understanding the intent, purpose, beauty and love behind every move of the Potter's hands, guiding us to realize our destined purpose and embrace the love of our creator.

I do not have all the answers to the unending questions in the world, but by nature, as humans, we have been wired to seek and search and we have been restless to find answers and looking for things beyond our understanding. I have named this thing in us that keeps looking for more: "The Searcher." We can find the searcher in all our lives, from education, careers, relationships and even our finances. Sometimes, people mistake this searcher in us for discontentment, but naturally, we want more and seek the unknown in hope, fear and love.

The needs of the searcher are endless, and we can never satisfy them all. However, if we master the art of contentment and position our lives in the hands of the potter, we can direct the searcher in us to seek the things that matter most before we go ashtray.

CHAPTER 1: THE TOUCH OF THE MASTER'S HANDS

Every masterpiece begins with a touch. When God, our Potter, lays his hands upon us, it is a touch filled with intention, direction, and infinite love. Just as clay feels the weight and pressure of the potter's touch, we also feel the guiding force of God molding us during times of hardship and growth.

This chapter delves into the spiritual journey shaped by God's touch. Just as an artist's masterpiece results from countless hours of dedication and passion, our souls are ceaselessly molded by the divine Potter, and in every touch, every press, every molding lies a story of love, purpose, and divine destiny.

As we move forward, let us remember that we are all under the benevolent guidance of the Master's hand

THE DIVINE PROCESS OF A SHAPING SOUL

The Gentle Initiation

Every great artwork and every remarkable creation, begins with a single touch. In spirituality, this touch is not physical—it is transcendent, meaningful, and immeasurable. As the eternal Potter, God never begins his work on us without purpose. Each touch is driven by profound intentions, steered in divine a direction, and soaked in boundless love.

The Weight of the Potter's Hand

Just as a potter must apply pressure to mold clay into a vessel, God applies pressures of life to mold us into spiritual masterpieces. These pressures come in various forms, including: challenges, trials, and the undulating rhythms of joy and sorrow. We sometimes feel burdened or crushed like clay. However, it's essential to remember that the intention is never to break but to shape, perfect, and fulfil a divine vision.

Sensing the Divine Direction

When clay is on a potter's wheel, it does not have the sight or sense of knowing its final form it will take. Similarly, we might only sometimes understand events that unfold in our lives. There are moments when we feel stretched, pinched, or flattened. However, with faith, we know that each experience, no matter how perplexing, is a purposeful stroke of the master's hands guiding us towards our destined shape.

Infinite Love in Every Touch

God's touch differs from that of any other. It is a touch filled with boundless love. Even when it feels heavy or challenging, it is always tempered with compassion and care. As the clay becomes a pot, it owes its form to both the gentle caresses and firm pressures of the potter. Similarly, our spiritual evolution is a blend of God's tender mercies and the lessons learned through challenges shaped by infinite love.

Embracing the Master's Vision

As we journey through life, there will always be doubts and despair. During such times, it helps to step back and envision ourselves not as mere clumps of clay but as divine works in progress. When we surrender to the touch of the master's hands and trust in His vision, we allow ourselves to be transformed into spiritual masterpieces, each unique and purposely designed.

CHAPTER 2: THE UNEXPECTED GIFT

Whispered Choices in Hushed Rooms

Two women sat in the dimly lit corridors of a hospital, and were lost deep in the conversation. One was a young mother-to-be aged 20 years, filled with fear and uncertainty about the future. The other, an older woman, was her mother-in-law who had seen many seasons of life, each with its joys and tribulations.

The young woman, with tears streaming down her face, spoke of the challenges she foresaw and felt unprepared for the journey of motherhood. The weight of responsibility and anticipated societal judgment was almost too much to bear.

"I don't think I can do this," she whispered.

Listening intently, the older woman, the family matrix, took a moment before speaking. Her voice was firm yet filled with love, "Life does not give us challenges we cannot handle. Sometimes, our biggest blessings come wrapped in trials."

<u>The Intercession of Love</u>

The grandmother spoke of her struggles, the moments when she felt defeated, and the power of perseverance that brought her through. She acknowledged her daughter's fear but reminded her of her strength. "Every child brings a new ray of hope, a fresh perspective to our lives. While I understand your fears, I see my potential. Not just in you, but in the life growing inside you."

She touched her daughter-inlaw's belly gently, feeling a faint flutter of life. "Give this child a chance, not just for them but for us —for you. Maybe this is the miracle we never knew we needed."

Moved by these words and the shared bond of experience, the young woman decided to change the course of her family's story.

A Legacy Of Hope

That child, saved from the brink, grew nurtured by the tales of resilience, love, and the grandmother's unwavering faith in life's potential. A close bond between the child and grandmother was evident to all who knew them.

They were two souls intertwined, a testament to the beauty of the second. That child would later grow to be living so that others may live; she would then be the reason someone could smile and write this book to contribute to the existing knowledge about God our Potter.

That child was me!

This was what my whole came about. I was almost aborted. Yes! It was evident in every shared laugh, lesson, and story that the decision made in that hospital corridor was not just one of preservation but one of profound love. The child, me, aware of this story, embraced life with vigor and gratitude that was infectious.

I chose to become a beacon of hope, not only for my family but for all who knew me, to live, to love and to enjoy, and to prove that every life has a purpose and every choice, a legacy.

CHAPTER 3: THE POTTER'S DESIGN

Each vessel has its own purpose. Some are designed for daily use, whereas others are designed for rare occasions. Similarly, God crafted each of us with a unique role in his design. By embracing our shape, we embrace the purpose God has set for us.

Every potter knows that before they mold the clay, they have a vision of final creation. The potter's hands lovingly shaped and sculpted the clay, applying the right amount of pressure to create the desired form. Similarly, God, the ultimate craftsman, shaped us purposefully. Similar to vessels on a potter's wheel, we have been carefully molded, not randomly or without thought, but with a precise vision in mind.

How often do we stop to think about this? How often do we

consider the intentional design that God has imprinted within us? If a vessel is unaware of its purpose, it may never truly understand its value, or why it was made the way it was.

<u>Embracing our Unique form</u>

Each of us, like these vessels, is crafted with care. Some of us like sturdy mugs designed for everyday use and comfort. Others may be like fine China, crafted for particular occasions or bearing intricate patterns. Some may feel that they resemble cracked pots, are imperfect and are flawed.However. they have a special purpose: to demonstrate that beauty can be found in imperfections and that purpose is not always about being flawless. I have come to have a clearer understanding and wisdom in this topic because of my experience studying molding and crafts at Achimota Basic School, Visual Arts class. I have envisioned my mold, sat behind a potter's wheel and felt what a potter feels thus, my understanding to all these.

By embracing our unique form and understanding our divine design, we can discover the essence of our purpose. For some, this might mean recognizing their calling as caregivers, nurturers, or providers. For others, this might mean using their voices to inspire change, tell stories, or lead communities. For some, their purpose might be to heal, learn, and grow, becoming a testament to resilience and strength.

The Journey to purpose

Finding my purpose has been a journey, not a destination. It's about listening to that inner voice, understanding my strengths and passions, and aligning them with the greater good. This journey has required me to step out of my comfort zones, face challenges, and even confront my deepest fear. But, in these moments of uncertainty, my true shape is revealed.

To live a life in alignment with God's purpose is to honour the craftsmanship with which we were made. It means being authentic to my design, regardless of how simple or complex it may seem. In a world that often values conformity, embracing our unique shape can be dauting. However, just as every vessel has its purpose, every individual plays a divine role in the tapestry of life. What, then defines value or purpose? Is there an intrinsic value in the universe without observers or conscious entities?God's design does not always concern what we can see on the surface. It goes deeper into core of our beings. By recognizing our value, understanding our design, and acting with intention, we fulfil our purpose and play our part in grand design.

Embracing the Unrecognized Gift

There is a saying about how we do not know where we will meet people in the future, so we have to be good for people. I believe that we should instead start playing our roles in the lives of others because that is wisdom and the right thing to do, and not because you are likely to meet someone in the future. That is also the basic form of purpose: "To live so that others may live."

This reminds me of the two shapes of purposes.

The first concerns living. It begins with this story of my maternal grandmother, whom I call my "smoothie Mary." Mary has always been known to people in my hometown as a very sober and peaceful lady, but she always talks about how life has dealt her an intricate hand, making her tougher. She believes that she has now understood the role she had to play in our lives.

Seeing us as her grandchildren makes her very proud, and she sees us as contributing to the world. Why? This is because my grandmother Mary had lost her twins at birth and still decided to go ahead and face the journey of bringing my other into this world.

She always wanted to be a police woman, but her dreams of becoming what she wanted were shattered when she had a huge sore on her left leg and had to end her schooling journey due to bullying. She could not afford basic school supplies or treat the sore with proper medication. One day, I asked her if she had any regret, and she replied, "I deeply regret not taking time to enjoy myself more. Instead, I worried a lot; if I knew what the world would gain through me, I would not have worried at all. I only wish for my dream house and a peaceful death now."

From my granny's reply, I can find the "searcher." wandering in at her age. The searcher in her would have wanted to have a dreamhouse, but she has mastered the art of contentment by showing me what she is most grateful for. I can now boldly testify that Smoothie Mary has lived so we may live.

The first purpose is knowing that the house you are building is not because of the present but because, in some years to come, your generation might not even remember your name and the investment you put into it or how you loved that color of the painting.

The second purpose is about the gift. Growing up, my home echoed with silence more than laughter. It was not the comforting kind of solitude that many find rejuvenating; it was the stinging loneliness that came from a disconnection within a family. The four walls around me witnessed my strained relationship with my father – a connection more like two parallel lines, always existing in the same plane, but never meeting.

It is a story that I hesitated to share for the longest time, thinking it was too specific and personal. However, over time, I realized that many bear the weight of unspoken words and unseen tears. We all have a story, a battle we are fighting in the confines of our hearts, and for me, it was the yearning for my father's understanding and approval.

In this environment, there was a glimmer of hope – a gift. A talent I knew existed within me, but like a firefly in daylight, it remained unrecognized and overshadowed by the prevailing gloom of my home life. I loved to sing. The melodies I created became my refuge, the lyrics of my unspoken words, and the rhythm of my heartbeat in a world that often felt cold and rhythmless.

However, my gift went unnoticed in a home where communication was sparse and my feelings were rarely shared.

You could not even think or choose anything for yourself without dictations or judgements. I didn't expect applause or recognition every time though. What I truly yearned for was understanding and connection. I hoped that through my songs, my heavenly and earthly father would hear the feelings I could not express, and that my talent would be a bridge to mend our strained relationship.

The years rolled on, and, while the gift within me yearned for light, shaping it took a backseat. Yet, I held on like a seed under the soil, waiting for rain. I believed in my gift even when the world around me seemed blind to it.

One fateful evening, an unexpected opportunity presented itself. Our local community hosted a talent show. Gathering my courage, I decided to participate, hoping that this would be my chance to let the world see the gift I knew I had.

The night of the performance, my heart raced. As I stood backstage, I saw my father in the audience. My emotions were a whirlwind of hope, fear, and longing. With a deep breath, I stepped onto the stage. As the music began and I sang my heart out, I felt an overwhelming sense of liberation. For those few minutes, I was free from the shackles of my strained past.

The applause that followed was heartwarming, but what truly touched my soul was seeing my father standing up, clapping, with tears in his eyes. That night, my gift was not just recognized; it began its journey of being shaped.

No, snap out of this, that stage performance never happened!

Life isn't a movie; it doesn't happen in a twinkle of an eye. Sorry to tell you, your grand future might not even be seen by the people that you want them to. At that point are you going to call yourself a failure? My father may never change, his words pierces the heart like a dagger and his aura never welcoming but I adjusted, and even though I still work on my gift, it isn't for recognition and approval's sake—instead, my situation made me realize the importance of seeing my gift as a calling and responsibility that needs to be executed.

I was enrolled in a boarding house at Achimota Basic School

from primary 5 to Junior High School. I hated coming home for vacations. There were times my dad would accuse me of being a witch, there were also times where he would slap and beat me and my brother till there were visible scars for a petty mistake like loosing my school socks. Till now I still have a scar on my right arm that no one knows how it came about.

There are simply no answers as to the many questions I have. To the extreme, this was my outlooking "lovely home." I am not writing this out of pain or anger but for you understand the magnitude of the scars I carry from my lived experience.

Do not worry or give up if you experienced a similar situation as mine, it is important to understand the weight of the journey of your purpose before anything else. I am sharing these scars of mine with you so that, you can also share yours in a better way and to help redirect the searcher in you, to a focus of purpose.

To all those who feel unseen and unheard. Let me remind you that you are the gift, you have a gift, not to prove anything but rather, to live. You need to polish and execute it no matter how hidden or suppressed you feel. Our purpose, our unique shape, might be buried under layers of pain, misunderstanding, or neglect. But with perseverance and faith, it can shine through, illuminating our lives and those around us.

THREADS OF FATE AND HANDS OF CREATION

<u>Clay in the Making</u>

Like every piece of clay that rests on a potter's wheel, the life of the child saved at the brink of existence, my life, began with uncertainty and wedlocks. The delicate balance between creation and void mirrored the decision made in that hospital corridor.

In the spiritual realm, God, the Master Potter, watches over every life. Just as the young mother was unsure about the shape and future of the life growing inside her, so did each piece of clay wait in anticipation to discover its purpose on the potter's wheel.

<u>Interventions of Wisdom</u>

Similarly, the potter who sees potential in every lump of clay, the grandmother, recognized the potential in the unborn life. With her guidance, akin to the Potter's skilled and deliberate hands, the young woman's life took a turn, setting the stage for a unique masterpiece to be crafted. The potter often uses tools, water, and pressure to shape the clay, ensuring it becomes a vessel of purpose. Similarly, the child's life was shaped by the nurturing stories of the grandmother, the knowledge of their unique beginning, and the lessons of life's unpredictability.

The Masterpiece Unveiled

As the child grew, their life began to resemble a beautifully crafted pot, each contour a testament to their unique journey, each pattern a reflection of their heritage. The resilience and hope they exuded were not just a product of their individual experience but also the legacy of the grandmother's wisdom and the divine design of the Master Potter.

I often reflected on my life's journey, realizing that, they were not just shaped by human hands but also by the divine touch of God. The challenges we faced, the love I received, and the purpose I discovered were all part of the intricate design planned by an eternal Artist.

I am constantly reminded by these events that my life is not just a series of random events. A divine hand is at play, guiding, shaping, and molding me, often through the wisdom and intervention of those who came before me. The hands that create masterpieces out of clay are the same that weave stories of hope, resilience, and purpose in our lives.

CHAPTER 4: THE SHAPE OF PURPOSE

Every vessel has a purpose. Some are designed for daily use, while others are for rare occasions. Similarly, God has created each of us with a unique role in His grand design. By embracing our shape, we embrace the purpose God has set for us.

Every potter knows that before they mold the clay, they have a vision of the final creation. The potter's hands lovingly shape and sculpt the clay, applying the right amount of pressure to create the desired form. Similarly, God, the ultimate craftsman, has shaped us purposefully. Like vessels on a potter's wheel, we have been care fully molded, not randomly or with out thought, but with a precise vision in mind.

Yet, how often do we stop to think about this? How often do we consider the intentional design God has im printed within us? If a vessel is unaware of its purpose, it may never truly understand its value or why it was made the way it was.

Embracing Our Unique Form

Like these vessels, each of us has been created with care. Some of us are like sturdy mugs designed for everyday use and comfort. Others may be like fine china, created for particular occasions and bearing intricate patterns. Some may feel they resemble cracked pots, imperfect and flawed. But even they have a special purpose: to demonstrate that beauty can be found in imperfection and that purpose isn't always about being flawless. By embracing our unique form and un der stand ing our divine design, we dis cover the essence of our purpose. For some, this might mean recognizing their calling as caregivers, nurturers, or providers. For oth ers, it might mean using their voices to inspire change, tell stories, or lead communities. And yet, for some, their purpose might be to heal, learn, and grow, be coming a testament to resilience and strength.

The Journey to Purpose

Finding our purpose is a journey, not a destination. It's about listening to that inner voice, understanding our strengths and passions, and aligning them with the greater good. This journey might require us to step out of our comfort zones, face challenges, or even confront our deepest fears. However, in moments of uncertainties, our true shape is revealed.

To live a life in alignment with God's purpose is to honour the craftsmanship with which we were made. It means being authentic to our de sign, no matter how simple or complex it may seem. In a world that often values conformity, it can be daunting to embrace our unique shape. But remember, just as every vessel has its purpose, every individual has a di vine role in the tapestry of life. What then defines value or purpose? Is there intrinsic value in a universe without observers or conscious entities?

God's design isn't always about what we can see on the surface. It goes deeper into the very core of our being. By recognizing our value, understanding our design, and acting with intention, we fulfil our purpose and play our part in the grand design.

<u>Embracing the Unrecognized Gift</u>

There's a popular saying in the Ghanaian Twi language about how we do not know where we will meet great people in future, so we have to be good to people in their "now." I believe the very moment we think in that direction, we lower our individual purpose to what we will gain from others in future

by being good to them. How about we instead, with wisdom, choose and start playing our roles in the lives of those we meet. This is because the purpose as a gift is recognizing that you have a role to play in the lives of those around you and everyone who encounters you, understand what life can really be even if it is their last day on earth. This is the right thing to do, not because you are likely to meet that person in future in an elevated status. Ultimately, a summation of the basic form of purpose: "To live so that others may live." This brings us to the two shapes of purpose. The first shape is about living. It begins with this story of my maternal grandmother, whom I call my "smoothie Mary." Mary has always been known to people in my hometown as a very sober and peaceful lady, but she told me about how life has dealt with her an intricate hand, making her tougher in the sense that, life may not see her as everyone sees. She believes she has now understood the role she had to play in our lives.

Seeing us as her grandchildren makes her very proud, and she sees us as a contributing factor to the world. Why? This is because my grandmother Mary before the birth of my mother who would have been her last born, had lost her twins at birth and still decided to go ahead and face the journey of bringing my mum into this world.

She had shattered dreams of becoming a police woman due to a huge sore she had on her leg from farming activities and with that, school had to come to an for her because she couldn't stand the stigma and bullying. She also couldn't afford basic school supplies or treat that sore with the proper medication. One day, I asked her if she had any regrets, and she

replied, "I deeply regret not taking time to enjoy more of my youthful days. Instead, I worried a lot; if I knew what through me the world would gain, I would not have worried at all. I only wish for my dream house and a peaceful death now."

From my granny's reply, we can find the " searcher. " wandering in there at her age. The searcher in her would have wanted to have a dream house, but she has mastered the art of contentment by showing me what she is most grateful for. With that, I am a waving flag of testimonies that smoothie Mary has lived so we may live.

The first shape of purpose is knowing that, that house you are building is not because of the present but because, in some years to come, your generation might not even remember your name and the investment you put into it or how you loved that colour of the wall painting so much.

The second shape of purpose is about the gift. Growing up, my home echoed with silence more than laughter. It wasn't the comforting kind of solitude that many find rejuvenating; it was the stinging loneliness that came from a peaceful wail, and disconnection within a family. The four walls around me witnessed my strained relationship with my father. A connection more like two parallel lines, always existing in the same plane, but never meeting. It's a story I hesitated to share for the longest time, thinking it was too specific and personal. But over time, I realized that many bear the weight of unspoken words and unseen tears. We all have a story, a battle we're fighting in the confines of our hearts, and for me, it was the yearning for my father's understanding and approval. I have fought within a battle of fear of being alone due to my past experiences. I have won my battle because of love and the understanding of purpose.

In this environment, there was a glimmer of hope – a gift . A talent I knew existed within me, but like a firefly in the daylight, it remained unrecognized and over shadowed by the prevailing gloom of my home life. I loved to sing. The melodies I created became my refuge, the lyrics my unspoken words, and the rhythm of the secret place in my heart beat in a world that often felt cold and rhythm less.

What I truly yearned for was an understanding and connection. I hoped that through my Gift, my father would hear the feelings I could not express, and that my talent would be a bridge to mend our strained relationship.

The years rolled on, and while the gift within me yearned for light, shaping it took a back seat. However, I held on like a seed under the soil , waiting for the rain. I believed in my gift even when the world around me seemed blind to it.

Then, one fateful evening, an unexpected opportunity presented it self. Our local community hosted a talent show. Gathering my courage, I decided to participate, hoping that this would be my chance to let the world see the gift I knew I had. The night of the performance, my heart raced. As I stood back stage, I saw my father in the audience. My emotions were a whirl wind of hope, fear, and longing. With a deep breath, I stepped onto the stage. As the music began and I sang my heart out, I felt an overwhelming sense of liberation. For those few minutes, I was free from the shackles of my strained past.

The applause that followed was heart warming, but what truly touched my soul was seeing my father standing up, clapping, with tears in his eyes. That night, my gift was not just recognized; it began its journey of being shaped.

No, snap out of this! That stage performance never happened!

Life isn't a movie; it is like it. The reality will disappoint and humble you. It doesn't happen in a twinkle of an eye. My father may never change, but I adjusted, and even though I still work on my gift, it isn't for recognition and approval's sake instead, it is a calling and a responsibility that needs to be executed.

To all those who feel unseen and unheard. Let me remind you that you are the gift , you have a gift , and you need to live; you need to polish and execute it no matter how hidden or sup pressed you feel. Our purpose, our unique shape, might be buried under layers of pain, misunderstanding, or neglect. But with perseverance and faith, it can shine through, illuminating our lives and those around us .

C

HAPTER 5: THE WHEEL OF LIFE (THE LIVED EXPERIENCE)

The potter's wheel constantly turns, keeping the clay centred. Our lives, too, have seasons – times of joy, sorrow, growth, and stagnation. We find balance amidst life's whirls by centring on God, our Divine Potter.

We each tread a path only we can see, and it is molded by many factors: our upbringing, the people we meet, the challenges we face, the triumphs we celebrate, and the tragedies we endure. This path, with its myriad twists, turns, ups, and downs, defines our "lived experience". No two paths are identical; they're as unique as the fingerprints on our fingers.

What is "Our lived experience?" This is every emotion, thought, and event we've encountered that creates the framework of who we are. It shapes our perceptions, attitudes, and reactions. But more importantly, it offers us the invaluable gift of perspective, teaching us empathy and understanding for others on their unique journeys.

Embracing Liberation and Learning from Mistakes

As the sun cast its warm glow on a new day, a young girl stood at the precipice of a new chapter in her life. Leaving the comfort and familiarity of home behind, she stepped into the vast, unknown expanse of the corners of the Ghana Institute of Journalism, away from the protective cocoon of her family. This wasn't just about pursuing education. For her, it was about freedom, exploration, and the glittering promises of self-discovery. This newfound freedom was heady and intoxicating. Suddenly, a young girl who grew up in Korlegonno had the world as her oyster, offering many choices and experiences. She felt liberated, unshackled from the constraints of her earlier life. Every day became an adventure and every encounter an opportunity.

But with great freedom came great responsibility, a lesson she was yet to learn. Mistakes were made. The allure of love, sometimes misplaced, led her down paths she hadn't envisioned.

Once a beacon of hope, academic choices now seemed like hasty decisions made in the euphoria of independence. She would sometimes miss lectures just to have nothing important to do and sleep all day at her hostel because of the new found freedom. With the excuse of being a bright student, she would focus on her love life that had nothing to offer over school. A love life that even her parents knew nothing about.

Yet, it is often in our darkest moments that we find our true selves. For me, it was faith that became my guiding star, my anchor in the stormy seas of doubt and regret. My lived experience, though fraught with mistakes, was also filled with lessons.

I realized my wrong choices weren't dead ends but detours that enriched my journey. Each mistake taught me resilience, each setback instilled in me a fierce determination to bounce back, and each heartbreak made my heart grow stronger, and I became more compassionate.

Through it all, my faith was unwavering. It reminded me that life wasn't about perfection but about growth.

<u>Embracing Our Unique Journey</u>

Like the young girl, we all have our chapters of liberation, mistakes, and growth. Our lived experience, while unique, resonates with universal truths of human existence. We will falter and err, but with faith and perseverance, we can reclaim our narratives and stride forward with renewed vigour.

As you navigate your Wheel of Life, remember that your experience is your most potent teacher. It offers you insights that no book or classroom ever can. Cherish it, learn from it, and most importantly, embrace it. Do not say that, because I was brought up this way or I went through this, I am accepting the way I am. There were times I thought I would hate men because of what I went through , but I then I looked at the sweet nature of my brother and saw something else.

The searcher in me always vibrated at a frequency of sweet things. I never had the mindset to treat anyone in a way that I have been treated. Not to be mistaken, I still look at my father with love and I even have his contact saved on my phone as "daddy my hero" This means a lot to me. Why? Because I needed a firehouse like my dad to shape the way I have become.

I have watched so many crime documentaries and the root of issues of most broken people in the stories, somehow begins with how they were brought up. This not to downplay anyone's scars but no matter how it began, it is not an excuse to do wrong. You can do it right.

For in the tapestry of life, it's not just the bright, vibrant threads that tell a story but also the dark, tangled ones. They unite to weave a tale of resilience, faith, and indomitable spirit. And that, you, dear reader, is the essence of the lived experience.

CHAPTER 6: EMBRACING THE PROCESS

The shaping process is only sometimes comfortable. The clay might yearn for relief as it is stretched, pressed, and turned. Our challenges and trials, similarly, are part of God's refining process, ensuring we become vessels of honour. The mid-afternoon sun was a glaring beacon as I stepped out of the (WASSCE) examination hall in 2016. I felt the weight of the world pressing down on me. Failure is a difficult pill to swallow, especially when you've given something your all. That day, as the result sheet revealed my score on the Core Math paper, the future looked daunting, almost unreachable.

Every individual has a moment in their life where they feel like they've been dropped into the deepest ocean, with the weight of their failures threatening to pull them down to the abyss. That was my moment. The paper I failed was not just any paper but a bridge to my dreams. It stood between me and my aspiration of making a mark in my chosen career.

"Why is this happening to me?" was the question I kept asking myself. I had prepared and studied, yet the outcome was far from what I had anticipated. But, as I would learn, life isn't always about immediate success. It's about the journey, the process, and the lessons learned.

In the quiet solitude of my room, as I reflected on my failure, an analogy came to my mind: "the process of molding clay". Clay, in its initial form, is just a lump. Unshaped, devoid of design. But patience, pressure, and time can transform it into a beautiful masterpiece. Similarly, this failure was just one part of a more extensive process, a part of my shaping.

My decision to rewrite the paper was no walk in the park. With the previous failure looming over me like a dark cloud, doubt and fear were constant companions. But there was also a glimmer of hope and determination. This was my second chance, and I had to make it count. As the first girl of my parents, I had always wanted to be a good example to my little sister who was born with a neurological disorder. I wanted to be a mark she can be proud of and look up to.

However, as I delved deeper into my preparations, the overwhelming feelings of anxiety returned. Was I setting myself up for another disappointment? Could I truly conquer this obstacle? With these thoughts swirling, I kneeled, praying fervently for guidance and strength. "God," I whispered, "take the wheel." At that point, the "Jesus take the wheel" song would have been on my playlist if I had a smartphone in those days.

The exam day came, and as I sat there, staring at the paper, something miraculous happened. The nervousness I had felt, the weight of my past failure, slowly started to lift when I saw my childhood studies teacher as my invigilator. There was clarity I hadn't felt before and some confidence and calmness in the atmosphere. The process brought me closer to my faith, and in that moment of absolute surrender, I felt an inexplicable peace. This is because I tapped into the mercy of God, practicing the words of "For a broken heart and a contrite spirit is what he desires"

When the results arrived, the joy and relief I felt were indescribable. I had passed! But this victory wasn't just about clearing a paper. It was a testament to the power of faith, resilience, and embracing the process.

Looking back, that failure in 2016 wasn't a setback but a setup for a grand comeback. It taught me the value of perseverance, the importance of faith, and the beauty of surrendering to a higher power. Like the clay that goes through intense molding to become a masterpiece, I, too, had undergone a refining process.

To anyone reading my story, know this: the shaping process isn't always comfortable. You will be stretched, pressed, and turned. You will face challenges that will make you question your path. Amidst all of that, remember that, these trials are part of God's refining process, ensuring you become vessels of honor.

Embrace the process, have faith, and you'll emerge stronger and wiser on the other side.

CHAPTER 7: THE KILN OF TRIALS (THE FIRE HOUSE)

After molding, the clay enters the kiln, also known as the (Fire House) where intense heat solidifies its form. Our trials are like this fire, solidifying our faith and commitment. They might be extreme, but they are necessary for our transformation.

The sun cast long shadows as I strode across the university campus, a place which had become a second home. But as I clutched the paper in my hand, its cold, stark reality contrasted sharply with the beautiful surroundings. The words seemed to glare back at me: "Statistics - Failed."

It wasn't a surprise, not really and not because I was not a bright student. Mathematics had always been a challenge. To me, numbers felt like an alien language that I had never quite grasped.

Whenever I faced a math problem, my mind fogged up, creating an insurmountable barrier because of how i grew reading almost everything and never really paying attention to numbers.

To the outside world, this was just another blip on an academic transcript. But to me, it symbolized so much more. This failure wasnt just a class or a subject I disliked, It was a testament to a more profound struggle quietly brewing within me. "How many times had I faced the flames of adversity and faltered?" So many question, many!

The image of a kiln came to mind - the "Fire House" where clay is put under intense heat to transform it. This trial, this failure, was my kiln.

As I sat beneath the old oak tree, its leaves rustling gently in the wind, I thought about how the clay must feel. It starts as something soft, malleable, and vulnerable. But as it enters the kiln, the flames dance around it, scorching and reshaping. During this process, the clay becomes solid, strong, and defined amid the fiery trials.

This process is both challenging and painless. The heat, the pressure, the intensity - all of it can be overwhelming. But it's necessary for the transformation. Like the clay, I was also being shaped by my trials. The failures, challenges, and disappointments were all part of my journey, molding me into the person I was destined to become.

I realized that I had a choice. I could see my failures as insurmountable challenges, as signs that I wasn't cut out for my chosen path. Or I could see them as necessary trials, essential for my growth.

Closing my eyes, I imagined myself as that piece of clay. I felt the heat, the pressure, and the pain. But I also felt the potential for transformation, the opportunity to emerge stronger and more resilient. At this moment, I embraced the kiln of trials, leaned into the heat, and trusted the process. I was determined not just to pass but to understand, to conquer the subject that had long been my nemesis genuinely, so why did I fail then?

The end of the semester arrived, with it, the final exam. My name wasn't on the diploma graduation class 2020 list because my results were still hanging. The next few months were a blur. I sought out help. I later learned this failure wasn't because I failed but because an assessment grade was missing. The thought of my experience had taken root within me, and I felt, to a point, that I failed again. A year on, I had a "Pass".

The journey through my kiln was not easy but had been transformative. My failure in statistics was not a testament to my inadequacy but a trial that helped shape me. The kiln had done its job. Standing tall on the university grounds, I realized that life would throw many more trials my way. But having faced the intense heat of this kiln, I felt prepared. This is because problems, much like the flames in a kiln, don't break us; they forge us.

CHAPTER 8: THE ARTIST'S VISION

The potter sees the finished product even before starting. God, too, has a vision for us, a hope, and a future. Trusting in His vision means believing that every touch, pull, and prod leads us to our destined shape. Indeed, every process begins with the intentions. Throughout the Bible, God constantly reminds us about—his intentions for humankind and his plans in every way. We are always assured that he knows what he sees and has the power to do.

What if we never existed? In our most challenging moments, we ask the most difficult questions. It reminds me of all my unanswered questions when facing something beyond my control and understanding. The purpose is not to create a perfect vessel but to engage in the beautiful, fulfilling act of creation itself. Some believe the problem of evil in a world supposedly governed by an all-loving, omnipotent deity is questionable. If we are all sculpted by this Potter for a specific, presumably benevolent purpose, how do we account for human suffering, frailty, and moral failings? While comforting, my metaphor in this book leaves room for contemplating whether the Potter is infallible or if the clay has attributes that even the Potter cannot fully control.

The existential crisis is not a reserved experience for the middle-aged or the elderly grappling with the specter of mortality. Rather, it is a universal phenomenon that can grip us at any stage of life, often when we least expect it. I was entangled in the complex web of existential dread quite early on.

From a young age, I found myself irresistibly drawn to profound questions beyond my years—questions about meaning, purpose, mortality, and the grand scheme of existence. This drive wasn't just mere childish curiosity but an intelligent manifestation of "The Searcher" within me. This innate searcher left me often pondering, "Why am I here?" or "What does it all mean?" amidst algebra homework and childhood games. Upon all the fufu and Ghana jollof, I was hungry!

Our society has various systems—education, religion, and culture—that attempt to provide us with a framework to make sense of our existence. Yet, these frameworks are often double-edged swords. On the one hand, they offer stability and answers; on the other, they can constrain our search for individual meaning, leading to existential unease.

For example, early indoctrination into a specific religious or philosophical belief provides an initial roadmap for understanding life. However, as we evolve and are exposed to multiple perspectives, the cracks in these once-solid foundations begin to appear. This unsettling revelation often catalyzes the existential crisis in our formative years, where we are just starting to grapple with our autonomy and the diversity of worldviews available.

From an evolutionary standpoint, questioning our environment and existence has been a survival mechanism, allowing us to adapt and evolve. Young minds are incredibly agile, constantly forming new neural pathways as they absorb information. This biological feature may make younger people susceptible to existential crises. They are biologically primed to question and seek, confronting fundamental uncertainties as they establish their identities.

The media and literature we consume also play a role. Works of existentialist philosophy, dystopian fiction, or even evocative music and art can trigger early-onset existential crises by exposing the fissures in society's constructed meanings.

Facing an existential crisis is reshaping and refining by the Divine Potter. These crises deepen our awareness and align us more closely with our destined purpose as they compel us to question, seek, and understand our existence's deeper currents. It's as if the Potter has momentarily loosened His grip, allowing the clay to wobble, only to be shaped into a more refined vessel.

The existential crisis, particularly when experienced early, is not merely a phase but a clarion call to engage deeply with our life's journey. In mastering the art of contentment and finding our place within the divine grand design, we can steer "The Searcher" in us towards more fulfilling pursuits. Mindfulness, deep reading, and existential therapy can offer solace and solutions.

While the timing of my existential crisis might have been unusually early, as at the age of thirteen years, the experience itself is a universal human endeavor. At some point, we all confront the haunting void of existential questions. These crises, disconcerting as they may be, serve as mile-markers on the highway of personal evolution. They invite us to pause, reflect, and often change course as we continue to craft our lives in the hands of the Divine Potter.

In the end, facing an existential crisis is not a pathology but a milestone in a life well-examined. It is a testament to our eternal worth and a call to realize the celestial significance of our existence, not just as creations but as co-creators in this intricate, beautiful tapestry of life.

So, as we sail through the existential seas of life, let us not forget our cherished position—continuously molded by divine hands for a celestial calling, all while steering our ship through tumultuous and calm waters. The existential crisis is not a storm to be avoided but a challenge to be navigated, an essential part of our eternal voyage.

The existential crises we face can be seen as moments when the Potter tests the flexibility and resilience of the clay. These moments define the final masterpiece, adding complexity and depth that an unexamined life could never achieve. Just as a potter must sometimes apply pressure or smooth out cracks to complete the envisioned form, existential crises are processes through which the Divine Potter refines and perfects us.

I mentioned the "Searcher" within us, constantly probing the depths of meaning, even during phases of our lives when we might seem too young for such hefty contemplations. This searcher is akin to the unformed clay on the wheel, full of potential, awaiting the potter's touch but also containing the essential elements that will define its final form within it. Here, the Searcher and the Divine Potter come into perfect synchrony, creating a masterpiece that is both predestined and yet infinitely malleable.

Additionally, I've touched on societal frameworks like education, religion, and culture as guiding posts and possible constraints. These are the external forces—the hands of multiple potters. However, they can introduce conflicting visions for what the final vessel should look like. Herein lies another layer of complexity: Are we a singular project of the Divine Potter, or are we communal works of art, continuously shaped by the hands of society, relationships, and self?

Thus, the existential crisis isn't a flaw in the design but a crucial stage in a sophisticated process of divine and self-craftsmanship. By navigating these crises, we become passive creations and active co-creators in the rich, complex tapestry of existence. We are both the clay and the potter, the created and the co-creator, forever intertwined in a celestial dance of will and destiny.

CHAPTER 9: THE BEAUTY IN IMPERFECTIONS

No pot is without imperfections. These quirks, rather than diminishing its value, make it unique. Our flaws, mistakes, and scars are testaments to our journey, and they tell a story of grace, redemption, and God's unending love.

In a world that constantly places the superficial on a pedestal, it's easy to be distracted by the glittering temptations that promise pleasure but deliver pain. Every soul on Earth has its own set of blemishes, its own set of mistakes. As believers, our faith journey is not about the absence of flaws but recognizing them and allowing God's transformative love to shine through them. Often, our lives echo the children of Israel. We've seen God's hand in our lives, delivering us from our personal Egypts, yet we find ourselves tempted by the golden calves of the world, chief among them the alluring trap of sexual desires that pull us away from the voice of God.

In times of vulnerability, the siren calls of the world, particularly sexual temptations, can be powerful. Just as Eve was enticed by the forbidden fruit in the Garden of Eden, believing it would make her wise, many of us are deceived by the allure of physical pleasure, thinking it might fill the void within. But the beauty of imperfections is that they are not a death sentence but a gateway to redemption.

I have met men who promised Ghc3000 monthly just so that I can strip myself naked for them. There are also others who just wanted to touch me so I could get whatever I want in the world from them. The strange thing about these demands is that, it happens when you are on the verge of something bigger coming your way wrapped in glittering advances.

When we stumble, fall prey to our desires and ignore God's voice, we might feel distant from His grace. But remember, God used broken people throughout history. David, a man after God's own heart, succumbed to the allure of Bathsheba. Yet, even in his deep sin, he found redemption when he returned to God with a repentant heart.

It is not too late, I have had my own share of it and it never ends well. Remember the signs, for that will show you that you are threading the right path. It's not the act of falling that defines us, but our choice to rise and seek His face again. God does not seek perfection; He seeks a heart willing to be molded, reshaped, and used for His glory.

Our imperfections, our moments of weakness, are opportunities for God to showcase His power and grace. Every scar, every flaw, every tear-streaked face can be a canvas on which God paints a masterpiece of redemption and restoration. The voice of God does not condemn us for our mistakes but beckons us closer to embrace His love, grace, and forgiveness.

In a society that celebrates the flawless, where filters and perfect angles are the norms, we must remember that God's Kingdom values the broken because it's through our cracks that His light shines the brightest.

These imperfections, born from ignoring God's counsel, became the stepping stones that allowed me to experience His grace in its most raw and redemptive form.

After my choices, God's unending love rescued me when I felt most alone, drowning in guilt and regret. The realization dawned that even when I turned a deaf ear to Him, His voice never wavered, never diminished, and never abandoned me.

The beauty of God's love is that it doesn't demand perfection. Instead, it seeks acknowledgement, repentance, and a heart willing to return to its Creator. My journey, dotted with the imperfections of my choices, became a testament to the boundless mercy and forgiveness God bestows upon those who turn back to Him. The parable of the prodigal son resonated with me more than ever; no matter how far we stray, God always waits with open arms to welcome us home.

In society, imperfections are often seen as liabilities, but in the spiritual realm, they are opportunities. Opportunities for growth, understanding, and deepening one's relationship with God. My failures became the milestones of my testimony, highlighting not my frailties but the relentless love of a Savior who redeems, restores, and rejuvenates. In retrospect, the voice I ignored was not silenced; it became louder, echoing with lessons of love, forgiveness, and redemption.

Today, I wear my scars not as symbols of shame but as badges of grace, reminders that God's love can transform, uplift, and heal even in the depths of despair. To those who find themselves at the crossroads, take a moment to listen to that still, small voice. But if you falter, remember that every imperfection and flaw is a chance to experience God's restored love's unparalleled beauty. Because in His hands, even the most broken vessel can be made whole again.

So, if you find yourself trapped by the chains of sexual demands or any other temptation that drowns out the voice of God, remember that your imperfections are not the end of your story. They are merely chapters in a greater narrative of grace and redemption. Draw near to God, and He will draw near to you. For in our weaknesses, His strength is made perfect.

In the end, it's not about the absence of imperfections but about the beauty and strength that can emerge from them when placed in the hands of the Almighty. The pot may have cracks, but it can

still hold the most precious of waters – God's unending love.

Chapter 10: The Vessel's Service

A vessel's true value is realized when it's put to use. We, too, are made to serve, to pour out love, kindness, and grace to others, reflecting the divine love that's been poured into us. A vessel's true value is realized when it's put to use. We, too, are made to serve, to pour out love, kindness, and grace to others, reflecting the divine love that's been poured into us.

For years, I grappled with finding my true calling. The pressures of modern life, the race to be the best, and the constant comparison to others often fogged my vision. Yet, amidst the blur, a single image kept reappearing - the sincere, radiant smile of a person who felt indeed seen, understood, and valued. That simple yet powerful gesture was what I was drawn to time and time again.

My little sister was born. She was born with a neurological disorder that affected her left-fingers' movement. This was a wakeup call to me. The importance of the vessel was not about a perfect physical looking vessel. It the unique presence of an individual, serving and walking the surface of the earth leaving its mark.

Upon introspection, it became clear. I realized my purpose was not merely to exist or to chase personal successes but to bring joy, even if fleeting, to those around me. Putting a smile on someone's face, especially in moments of darkness, was a balm to their soul and mine. The ripple effect of that moment of happiness, the cascade of positive emotions it set off, made it all worthwhile. The value of such a gesture was immeasurable.

And so, "The Smilespiration Project" was born. An NGO dedicated to spreading cheer, positivity, and, above all, smiles. It was not about physical acts or monetary help and genuine human connections. The goal was to touch lives of deprived children, listen to stories, understand pain, and offer hope. The Smilespiration Project aimed to ensure that no one felt alone in their struggles through various initiatives like community events, workshops, and counselling sessions.

The stories I encountered were both heart-wrenching and inspiring. The need for love and understanding was universal, from children in orphanages to elders in homes, people experiencing homelessness on the streets, and those battling mental health issues. Each smile we brought about was a testament to the project's mission, each story a thread woven into the tapestry of our shared human experience.

The vessel of my being found its true service. By establishing The Smilespiration Project, I discovered that my life's value wasn't gauged by personal achievements but by the lives I touched and the joy I spread. Every smile became a confirmation that in serving others, in being a vessel of love and kindness, I was fulfilling my purpose.

Being a part of something bigger than oneself is a humbling experience. Every day, I'm reminded of the immense power and responsibility of understanding one's true purpose. I am merely a vessel, but even a simple vessel can change the world when filled with meaning and love.

And as The Smilespiration Project grew, so did its reach and impact. The simple idea that began as a personal calling soon became a movement, proving that the universe conspires to magnify your efforts when you find your purpose and serve with all your heart.

I urge everyone to look deep within, to find their purpose, and to understand the value they bring to this world. In service, love, and kindness, we find our true selves and leave a legacy that outshines any personal accolade. And always remember, the brightest light is that which shines for others.

CHAPTER 11: THE JOY OF THE POTTER

The potter rejoices in the completion of his work. Similarly, God takes delight in us, not because of our perfection, but because we are his creation, made in his image, reflecting His glory.

Amidst the vast stretches of a tranquil village, the rhythmic humming of the potter's wheel echoed like a lullaby, intertwined with the gentle murmurs of nature. As dawn painted the sky, the potter sat at his wheel, hands gently molding and shaping the clay daily. The process was not just an act of creating for him but a profoundly spiritual journey.

The potter, Samuel, believed every simple or intricate creation carried a part of his soul. Each pot, plate, or vase was a testament to his dedication, patience, and love for his craft. While the outside world chased perfection, Samuel cherished the imperfections in his creations, for they told stories, holding memories of his gentle touches and occasional hesitations.

One day, as the sun descended, casting a golden hue over the village, Samuel completed a pot unlike any other he had made before. It wasn't the largest or most ornate, but it held a unique charm. His heart swelled with an inexplicable joy as he set it down to dry. It was as if this pot held the essence of every lesson he had learned, every joy he had felt, and every challenge he had overcome in his journey as a potter.

As children from the village gathered around, one of them, a curious little girl named Lila, asked, "Why does this pot make you so happy, Samuel? It looks like the others you've made before."

With a soft smile, Samuel replied, "Lila, every creation has its spirit. Just as parents rejoice in their children, not because they're without flaws, but because they see a part of themselves in them, I rejoice in this pot. Not for its perfection, but because it reflects my journey, my soul."

An old wise woman, known for her tales of the divine, had been listening. She added, "Just as Samuel finds joy in his creation, so does the Creator rejoice in us. God doesn't look for our perfection. He cherishes us because we are His creation, sculpted with care and imbibed with a spark of His divine spirit. Just as the pot is made in Samuel's image, bearing the mark of his hands and the warmth of his touch, we too are made in God's image, reflecting His infinite glory."

Under the canopy of the twilight sky, the villagers looked at each other with a newfound appreciation. The pot, gleaming in the dying light, served as a profound reminder of their worth in the grand tapestry of creation. Each of them, with their imperfections, dreams, and stories, was a unique masterpiece in the eyes of the divine.

From that day, Samuel's pot took a place of pride in the village square, not just as an object of beauty but as a symbol of divine love, the connection between the Creator and His creations, and the eternal dance of joy and gratitude.

Just as Samuel's creations are in his image, bearing the unique imprints of his hands and spirit, we are reflections of our Creator. We carry the divine signature within us, not in our perfection, but in our essence, our very being."

The pot, already symbolic, becomes even more meaningful, emphasizing that every individual, irrespective of their flaws, is a testament to God's love and creative power.

CHAPTER 12: THE ETERNAL PROMISE

The potter's desire isn't just to create a vessel and cherish it forever. God desires to have an eternal relationship with us. His love, guidance, and promises are unending, and He longs for us to embrace our role as His beloved creation.

One can discern the symphony of creation in the stillness of the potter's workshop. The whisper of the spinning wheel, the subtle press of fingers shaping the clay, and the anticipation of a formless lump of clay transforming into a masterpiece. The same dance of creation can be found in our lives as God molds and shapes us, every push and pull an act of love, guiding us towards our highest purpose. This is the eternal promise: that in every moment, in every challenge and joy, God is at work, creating a story of beauty and purpose out of our lives.

The Searcher within us, that restless spirit always seeking more, often misleads us to believe that the only way to find purpose is by relentlessly chasing after things of this world: the next job promotion, a bigger house, or the ideal romantic relationship. Yet, these pursuits are mere threads in the grand tapestry of our existence. They might add colour and texture but are only part of the story.

The Searcher is a gift, a divine compass planted within our souls, urging us to quest for the eternal and the infinite. It nudges us beyond the temporary and vast expanse of God's love. When we let God be the potter and ourselves the clay, we find that the Searcher's true purpose is to seek an everlasting connection with our Creator, to discover our place in His grand design.

Living purposefully isn't about silencing the Searcher or suppressing our desires. It's about redirecting that powerful force towards what truly matters. Instead of searching for temporary joys and fleeting achievements, we should strive to understand God's plan for us. What does He desire for our lives? How can we align our pursuits with His purpose?

When we surrender ourselves to the Divine Potter, we understand that every challenge, every setback, is a shaping, a molding to make us into vessels worthy of His eternal promise. Instead of feeling resentful by life's ebbs and flows, we begin to see them as necessary processes, refining us and making us stronger and more aligned with our purpose.

In every moment of doubt or darkness, when we feel lost or aimless, the Searcher within can find solace in the eternal promise of God's love. We must remember that our purpose isn't just about individual achievements or worldly accolades. It's about fulfilling God's role for us, being a beacon of His love, and helping others find their way to Him.

As we move forward, let the Searcher in us not be distracted by the world's glittering promises but be drawn towards the eternal light of God's love and purpose. Let us not merely be vessels shaped by the Potter but become vessels overflowing with His grace, love, and promise.

Ultimately, the eternal promise is not about what we can gain in this life but about the legacy we leave and the connection we forge with our Creator. Let us embrace the Potter's Desire and, in doing so, find the true purpose of the Searcher within us.

A LIFETIME OF SHAPING

As you journey through life, may you find joy in each touch of clay, each spin of the wheel, and each moment in the kiln. May you be a conscious, purposeful potter, crafting a masterpiece that reflects your highest vision for a life well-lived. "The Potter's Desire" is a testament to God's endless love, patience, and vision for each of us.

As we sail through the voyage of existence, let's never forget our cherished position — cradled in the hands of the Supreme Craftsman, continuously molded, honed, and chiselled for a celestial calling. Engage with the journey, have faith in His grand design, and take heart in realizing our eternal worth and love in His eyes.

The clay is but an extension of your essence. Your choices give it form, while your spirit infuses it with meaning.

Happy Crafting!

To my dear late grandmother, Mercy Adwoa Peprah, Whom I was named after, this book is dedicated to you. You believed in me when no one else did. I will forever be grateful for that. Even though you are no longer with us, your memory lives on in my heart and this book.

To my little sister, Lovia Koah, you are intelligent, bold and beautiful.

To the first fruit of my womb, I think about you a lot and the journey ahead of you, a motivation to leave behind something valuable. Thank you for everything.

ACKNOWLEDGEMENT

I acknowledge the inspiration and wisdom of God, who blessed me with the ability to write and share my ideas with the world. I would like to express my deep gratitude to all those who contributed to the creation of this book. This book would also not have been possible without the love and support of Daniel Kofi Mensah, who motivated me when I felt like quitting. I am profoundly grateful to the editors and publishers of this book.

ABOUT THE AUTHOR

Mercy Peprah Asare

Meet a young and vibrant woman who enjoys sharing her intimate walk with God. She recently graduated with a Bachelor's Degree in Public Relations from the Ghana Institute of Journalism, now known as UNiMAC-GIJ. She also holds a Diploma in Communication studies from the same institution. In addition to her academic achievements, 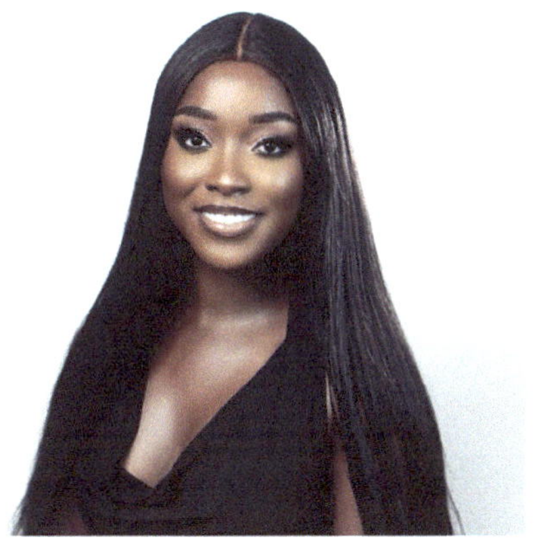 she has participated in two prestigious pageants in Ghana, Miss Malaika Ghana and Miss Ghana.

Aside from her academic and pageant achievements, she is also the founder of the Smilespiration Project, an NGO in Ghana that aims to bring smiles to the faces of underprivileged children and find sustainable ways to address their plights.

Mercy is a multi-talented individual who loves to compose songs and play the keyboard. She is also an entrepreneur in the field of makeup artistry, where she showcases her dancing skills. She truly is a lady with many hats.

BOOKS BY THIS AUTHOR

The Potter's Desire

"The Potter's Desire" explores the intricate relationship between human free will and divine purpose through the lens of the ancient parable of the Potter and the clay.

In this seminal work, the author introduces "The Searcher" as an innate aspect of the human condition, reflecting our perpetual quest for meaning across various facets of life, including education, careers, relationships, and finances. However, this restless searching often risks leading us astray unless we learn the art of contentment and understand our place in the hands of the Divine Potter—God.

The book takes its readers on a transformative journey to master this delicate balance, advocating for a life of purposeful shaping and reshaping.